EDGE BOOKS

TRUE TALES OF SURVIVAL PRESENTS:

STRANDED!

AMY RACINA'S STORY OF SURVIVAL

by Tim O'Shei

Consultant:
Al Siebert, PhD
Author of *The Survivor Personality*

Capstone
press

Mankato, Minnesota

Edge Books are published by Capstone Press,
151 Good Counsel Drive, P.O. Box 669, Mankato, Minnesota 56002.
www.capstonepress.com

Library of Congress Cataloging-in-Publication Data
O'Shei, Tim.
    Stranded!: Amy Racina's story of survival / by Tim O'Shei.
    p. cm.—(Edge books. True tales of survival)
    Summary: "Describes how hiker Amy Racina survived a fall in the Sierra Nevada
mountains"—Provided by publisher.
    Includes bibliographical references and index.
    ISBN-13: 978-1-4296-0088-0 (hardcover)
    ISBN-10: 1-4296-0088-8 (hardcover)
    1. Rock climbing accidents—California—Kings Canyon National Park—Juvenile
literature. 2. Wilderness survival—California—Kings Canyon National Park—Juvenile
literature. 3. Racina, Amy, 1956– —Juvenile literature. I. Title.
GV199.42.C22K56597 2008
796.52'23092—dc22   2006102269

Editorial Credits
Angie Kaelberer, editor; Jason Knudson, set designer; Kyle Grenz, book designer,
    Scott Thoms, photo researcher; Kelly Garvin, photo stylist

Photo Credits
Amy Racina, 4, 8, 13, 22, 25, 27, 29 (all foreground)
Capstone Press/Karon Dubke, 14, 20 (both foreground)
Lucky Oliver/Aaron Johnson, front cover
Shutterstock/Bryan Brazil, back cover, 18–19, 32; Cecilia Lim H M, 16–17;
    Chee-Onn Leong, 1, 12–13, 14–15, 24–25 (all background); Mike Norton,
    10–11, 30–31; Peter Weber, 2–3; Sarah Scott, 6–7, 20–21, 28–29
    (all background); Sebastien Burel, 4–5, 22–23 (both background);
    Steven Bourelle, 26–27 (background)

**Capstone Press gratefully thanks Amy Racina, www.angelsinthewilderness.com,
for sharing her story and providing photos for this book.**

1 2 3 4 5 6 12 11 10 09 08 07

TABLE OF CONTENTS

ONE STEP TO DISASTER

4

Amy was excited to begin her hiking trip in the summer of 2003.

LEARN ABOUT:

- **Peaceful hike**
- **On the edge of a cliff**
- **Bone-breaking fall**

In the summer of 2003, Amy Racina hiked alone through the Sierra Nevada Mountains in California. She planned her trip to last 17 days.

Amy loved the wilderness. The towering trees, glistening lakes, and steep slopes were peaceful and relaxing. Hiking gave Amy the chance to think about important things, like her job, her son, and her future.

August 4 was the 12th day of Amy's trip. She hiked into Tehipite Valley in Kings Canyon National Park. Hikers rarely entered Tehipite, where the steep and rocky trails were dangerous even for an experienced hiker.

At one point, Amy lost the trail. To get back to the trail, she needed to make her way across a steep hill. She clutched a tree and a rock to keep her footing.

Suddenly, the ground broke out from under her. Amy lost her grip. She felt her body falling. The rocky ground below rushed toward her. She thought to herself, "So this is how it ends."

Amy's body crunched against the rocky bottom of a ravine. Her bones shattered. Her flesh tore.

Amy's peaceful hike was now a life-and-death challenge.

Amy thought, "So this is how it ends."

Amy fell after she lost the trail she was following.

CHAPTER 2

SOLO HIKER

LEARN ABOUT:

- Love of hiking
- California life
- Going solo

Amy took her first hike at age 16 with her brother and dad.

Amy started hiking in 1972, at age 16. Amy, her father, and her 13-year-old brother, Daniel, drove 3,000 miles (4,800 kilometers) from their home in Maryland to Sequoia National Park in California.

Amy was nervous. She wasn't sure she could handle several days of tough hiking. On the first day, Amy and her family hiked about 11 miles (18 kilometers). Her muscles ached. She could barely keep her backpack on her shoulders. The next day brought more of the same. So did the day after that.

The hike was exhausting. But with each day, Amy felt her body getting stronger. She also appreciated the beauty of her surroundings. By the end of the 46-mile (74-kilometer) trip, Amy realized that the strength and peace she felt in the wilderness was something she could never experience at home. She was hooked on hiking.

A CALIFORNIA MOVE

When Amy was 24, she moved from Maryland to California. Using her skills as a writer and designer, she worked at a variety of jobs. Eventually, she started two small companies. One was Instant Pool Cards™, which printed and sold game cards. The other was a traveling store called The Everyday Goddess™. Amy set up a booth at fairs to sell clothes and gift items.

By the time Amy was 35, she was divorced and had a son named Sam. When Sam was small, Amy took him on hiking trips. By age 15, though, Sam had lost interest in hiking. But Amy still loved the outdoors. She began to plan longer trips. Her biggest ever was to be an August 2003 hike through Kings Canyon in the southern Sierra Nevada Mountains. The trip would take 17 days and cover about 170 miles (274 kilometers). Sam, then 16, would stay with his father. Amy planned to take the hike alone.

Kings Canyon National Park covers 461,901 acres (186,931 hectares) of the Sierra Nevada Mountains.

LONE HIKER

Amy had been taking solo hikes for 20 years. Her father had taught her that if she was well prepared, she could stay safe while hiking alone. Plus, Amy enjoyed the privacy. Solo hiking gave her the energy to deal with everyday life.

For most of the first nine days of Amy's Kings Canyon trip, she hiked in areas where other hikers traveled. Some days, she saw as many as 50 people. Amy stopped and chatted with many of them. Though she enjoyed the conversations, Amy was anxious for more privacy.

On day nine, Amy veered off the popular trails and into lesser-known parts of the forest.

Without the company of other people, she noticed small, beautiful details. Amy enjoyed looking at a patch of colorful flowers or spying on small creatures.

The trip was as wonderful as Amy had hoped—until day 12. That's when her dream trip came to a crashing halt.

Early in her trip, Amy stopped at the John Muir Memorial Shelter in Kings Canyon.

13

CHAPTER 3

INCH BY INCH

LEARN ABOUT:

- Bloody injuries
- Survival strategies
- Whistling for help

14

Amy used a silk scarf similar to this one to stop the bleeding from her knee.

When Amy landed in the ravine, she was grateful to still be alive. But the 60-foot (18-meter) fall had shattered her body. Her nose was broken, her front tooth was gone, and her fingers sprained. Amy's left hip was broken in two places. Both legs were broken, and her right ankle was dislocated.

Worst of all was Amy's right knee. It was mangled and bloody, with the bones jutting out. A hole the size of a fist revealed the crushed kneecap. Amy realized that she was losing blood quickly. At this rate, she would die.

Luckily, Amy's backpack had landed just a few feet from her. She used a silk scarf to tie a tourniquet around her leg and slow the bleeding. Then she took a small bottle of hydrogen peroxide and poured it into her knee. The peroxide would help kill germs in the wound.

Soon, Amy began shaking. She realized that she was going into shock. That's when she remembered a lesson her mother taught her: chicken soup makes everything better. Amy pulled out her pot and propane stove to make chicken soup. The hot soup warmed up Amy and stopped her shaking. She covered herself with her sleeping bag and fell asleep.

CHOOSING TO SURVIVE

At first, Amy thought she would die. She felt at peace, knowing her body would become part of the mountains she loved so much. But that thought didn't last long. Soon, Amy made a key decision. She was going to survive. She had enough food to eat for a few more days, and also knew that the human body can go for weeks without food. Water was more important. Luckily, a stream trickled nearby.

EDGE FACT

Shock is caused when too little blood is flowing through the body. People in shock can die within hours.

As the sun set over the mountains, Amy decided she was going to fight for her life.

Amy had to cross water as she tried to get to the trail.

18

Amy's injuries were more urgent. Amy knew infection could come on fast. She kept an eye on her leg for shooting red streaks, which were a sign of blood poisoning. She saw none.

Amy had fallen in a part of Kings Canyon where hikers rarely traveled. The chance of someone passing by was small. She hadn't brought an emergency whistle, and cell phones don't work in the wilderness. Plus, Amy's friends and family expected her to be gone several more days. Nobody would be looking for her.

INCHING FORWARD

Amy wanted to get closer to the main trail, which was about 2 miles (3.2 kilometers) below where she lay. Since she couldn't stand, she used her hands to scoot forward in a sitting position. She tied her backpack to her waist with a rope and dragged it behind her.

The process was painful and slow. It got worse when she came upon a freezing pool of water that was 3 feet (.9 meter) wide and about 18 inches (46 centimeters) deep. Amy wrapped her sleeping bag and extra clothes in a plastic bag and slid into the pool. Crossing it was easier than getting out. Amy nearly passed out as she struggled to pull herself from the water.

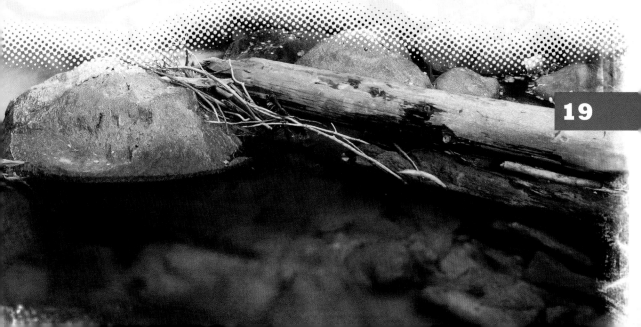

"Help me! I have broken legs!"

Amy cut a hole in a water jug to make a megaphone.

CRIES FOR HELP

After three days, Amy had traveled less than 250 feet (76 meters). A large boulder and trees blocked her from going any farther. Her right knee was becoming infected, and she knew she wouldn't survive much longer alone.

Ever since her fall, Amy had been yelling for help. She heard nothing in return. As she lay trying to think of what to do next, she yelled again. "Help me! I have broken legs!"

In the distance came two faint toots on a whistle.

Amy grabbed an empty water jug and cut a hole in it with her Swiss Army knife. She used the bottle like a megaphone to make her voice louder.

Along with the whistles, Amy now heard voices. She kept yelling, trying to direct them toward her. But suddenly, both the voices and the whistles stopped. Had Amy missed her only chance of rescue?

CHAPTER 4

MOUNTAIN RESCUE

Jake stayed with Amy until
the rescuers came.

After the whistles stopped, Amy felt the deepest despair since her fall. She couldn't understand how she could come so close to being rescued, and then have the hope yanked away.

Suddenly, Amy heard a person scrambling down the slope. The rescuer's name was Jake Van Akkeren. Jake had been hiking with his wife, Leslie Bartholic, and their friend Walter Keiser. Jake cleaned Amy's wounds and spent the night by her side. Walter and Leslie set up a camp in a meadow near the ravine. The next day, Walter ran 10 miles (16 kilometers) until he found a group of firefighters on vacation.

One of the firefighters rode a horse 10 miles to his car, where he used a shortwave radio to call for help. Within hours, park rangers Debbie Brenchly and Fred Mason arrived in the ravine. The rangers saw how severe Amy's injuries were. If they didn't get her quickly to a hospital, she could lose her infected right leg.

RAISED FROM THE RAVINE

The rangers talked about ways to get Amy out of the ravine. They could try to carry her, but the steep, rocky slopes would make that extremely dangerous. Even if they could carry her, it would take too long.

The rangers settled on having a helicopter lift Amy from the ravine. Early on the evening of August 8, a rescue helicopter arrived and hovered overhead. There was no room for the helicopter to land. Instead, a person inside the helicopter lowered a cable attached to a large basket.

Amy was frightened about the idea of dangling in a basket. But it was the best way to get her out of the ravine. The rangers packed Amy into the basket. The helicopter pilot slowly lifted her upward.

Amy squeezed her eyes shut and counted inside her head. After counting to 100 four times, she opened her eyes. The dangling flight was over. She was in a clear area being loaded into a medical helicopter. That helicopter would fly her to a hospital.

EDGE FACT

Amy believes the hikers who rescued her were the only ones who went by in a week.

25

This rescue helicopter flew Amy to safety.

GETTING HEALTHY

Doctors at the University Medical Center in Fresno treated Amy for dehydration and performed several surgeries. They put metal plates in her hip. A graft of skin and muscle was used to repair her knee. The doctors told Amy she was rescued just in time. One more day, and the infections would have reached her organs. That probably would have killed her.

After the accident, Amy became closer to her son, Sam. They began talking more openly. Sam told his mom that he loved her. He also helped out by doing household chores and going to the grocery store.

EDGE FACT

Amy had no medical insurance, and her hospital bill came to $300,000. Eventually, the state of California paid all but $11,000 of the bill.

Amy's son, Sam, helped her through her recovery.

HIKING AGAIN

Amy steadily recovered during the next year. Several months after her accident, Amy was in a grocery store when a woman recognized her. The woman asked Amy about her fateful hiking trip, saying, "You won't be doing that again, will you?"

Amy's answer was yes. Once she recovered, Amy could walk, swim, and ride her bike. She tired more quickly than before, but had no intention of giving up her lifelong love of hiking. In May 2005, she took a solo hike in Kings Canyon.

That year, Amy published a book about her accident, *Angels in the Wilderness*. She also shares her story through speeches and interviews.

Amy tells audiences that she survived because she stayed calm and never gave up. She didn't lie at the bottom of the ravine and feel sorry for herself. Instead, she focused on tasks she could do, like eating, treating her wounds, and using her hands to inch forward.

She could have given up, but she never viewed that as a choice. Amy's positive attitude helped her survive.

Today, Amy is still hiking and enjoying the wilderness.

29

GLOSSARY

graft (GRAFT)—body tissue that is removed from one part of the body and used to repair another part

ranger (RAYN-jur)—a person in charge of a park or forest

ravine (ruh-VEEN)—a deep, narrow valley with steep sides

shock (SHOK)—a medical condition caused by a dangerous drop in blood pressure and flow; people suffering from shock can die.

tourniquet (TUR-nuh-ket)—a tight wrapping used to prevent a major loss of blood from a wound

READ MORE

Hall, Margaret. *Yosemite National Park.* Symbols of Freedom. Chicago: Heinemann, 2006.

Markle, Sandra. *Rescues!* Minneapolis: Millbrook Press, 2006.

O'Shei, Tim. *The World's Most Amazing Survival Stories.* The World's Top Tens. Mankato, Minn.: Capstone Press, 2007.

INTERNET SITES

FactHound offers a safe, fun way to find Internet sites related to this book. All of the sites on FactHound have been researched by our staff.

Here's how:

1. Visit *www.facthound.com*

2. Choose your grade level.

3. Type in this book ID **1429600888** for age-appropriate sites. You may also browse subjects by clicking on letters, or by clicking on pictures and words.

4. Click on the **Fetch It** button.

FactHound will fetch the best sites for you!

INDEX